Copyright © 2015 Rising Son International, Ltd.

All rights reserved. No part of this book may be reproduced without written permission from the Publisher

First Edition

Guthrie, Arlo

Summary: A beloved moose roams the Berkshire hills and becomes a legend

ISBN: 978-0-9915370-9-9

Manufactured in China by C&C Joint Printing Co., (Guang Dong) Ltd. in April 2015

Rising Son International, Ltd.
Washington, MA
USA

# OLD BILL
## The Famous Berkshire Moose
### Or
### He's Just Ahead in Pittsfield

### By Arlo Guthrie
### Illustrations by Kathy Garren

Rising Son International, Ltd.

# Dedication

Around our small town of Washington, Berkshire County, Massachusetts, there is a large state forest called "October Mountain State Forest." In 1915 the 11,000+ acre game preserve was purchased by the State of Massachusetts from the estate of William C. Whitney (1841-1904), who was Secretary of the Navy during the administration of President Grover Cleveland. The park area has grown over the years and is now the largest state forest in Massachusetts.

After William Whitney's death, most of the exotic animals he'd imported into the preserve were relocated, but one escaped into the wild. Sometime during the transition from game preserve to state forest a young moose got away, and Game Warden William W. Sargood from Lee, Mass. maintained a friendly relation with the escapee. The young moose was named after the warden, becoming known as "Old Bill."

When well-known critic and author Walter P. Eaton (1878 - 1957) wrote an essay entitled "The Odyssey Of Old Bill - The Famous Berkshire Moose," the moose became instantly famous. Eaton had written a number of nature articles relating to The Berkshires, and the piece immortalized Old Bill.

During the hunting season of 1920 in the nearby town of Otis, Massachusetts, a man evidently mistook the famous moose for a deer and killed him. Warden Sargood himself saved Old Bill's head for posterity, having it mounted and put on display at The Berkshire Museum in Pittsfield, Massachusetts.

In the early Fall of 1969 I purchased an old farm just down a dirt road from the former game preserve. It'd been just under 50 years since Old Bill roamed the woods we've called home ever since. Prior to the 75th anniversary of Old Bill's passing, I was asked to write an introduction for a reprint of Walter Eaton's Odyssey of Old Bill. I happily did so in the form of a simple poem.

Within a few years from the first publication of this book, Old Bill will have been a resident of The Berkshire Museum for over a century. In preparation for that event, this book is written with gratitude to The Berkshire Museum and lovingly dedicated to the memories of Warden William W. Sargood and Old Bill - The Famous Berkshire Moose.

Arlo Guthrie
Washington, Massachusetts

I'm going to see a friend of mine
Old Bill was once his name

He roamed the woods of Washington
A moose of note and fame

In Walter Eaton's Odyssey
The Chronicles retell

Of how Bill grew to be the Bull
Moose that we loved so well

Bill was born upon the mountain
Long before the roads were paved

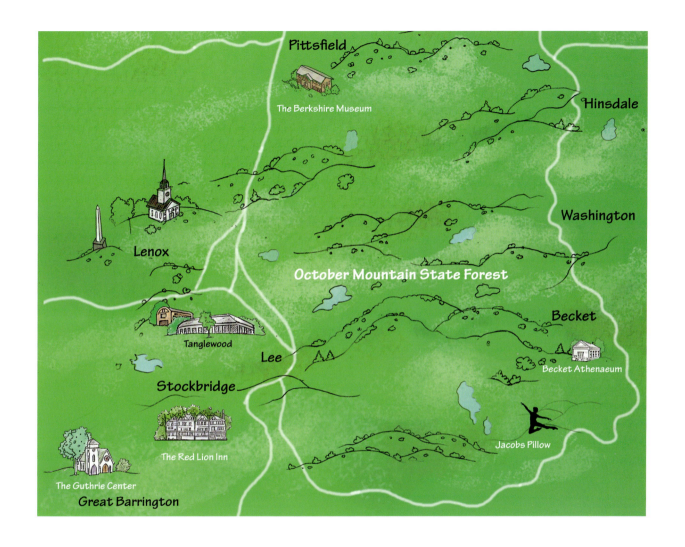

In a part of Massachusetts
That a guy named Whitney saved

For William Whitney set aside
What we have come to call

October Mountain Forest
You should see it in the Fall

They say that as the years went by
Old Bill became well known

The locals called his whereabouts
To neighbors on the phone

He visited the towns around
And never learned to fear

He waltzed right into Lenox
Though I can't recall the year

His end came unexpectedly
A hunter brought him down

He thought he'd killed a deer, instead
Old Bill lay on the ground

They brought Old Bill to Pittsfield
He's there in the museum

His face is mounted on the wall
Where you can go and see 'im

And that's just where I am going
For Old Bill was once alive

And the number of the years gone by
Have passed seventy-five

And I think I've come to know him
'Bout as much as I e'er will

That's why I wrote this poem
For the moose we called Old Bill